PRESENTING
ATAHUALPA YUPANQUI

16 Solos arranged for Low G Ukulele

DAVE BROWN

Dedicated to finger-picking Ukulele players everywhere

The ukulele: a noble little instrument; an irritating little instrument. Both views are valid, but for millions of people around the world, the ukulele is fast becoming as instrument of desire.

— WILL GROVE-WHITE —

Member of Ukulele Orchestra of Great Britain

CONTENTS

TUNES

FURTHER READING

INTRODUCTION

I came across the melodic guitar music of Atahualpa Yupanqui while researching music from Latin America.

The distinctive South American indigenous quality of these simple tunes impressed me. As I researched further into this extraordinary person, the more of his music, I wanted to play.

Atahualpa Yupanqui, whose real name was Héctor Roberto Chavero Aramburu, was born in the Argentine pampas, nearly 200 kilometres from Buenos Aires. His mother was from the Basque region of Spain and his father was of Quechua (aboriginal South American) origin.

Early in his career, he adopted the Quechua stage name Atahualpa Yupanqui, which combines the names of two legendary Incan Kings.

His first jobs of delivering telegrams and delivering goods by mule allowed him to travel. On his travels, he collected and sang folk songs.

Travelling became his life. He spent time in the rural northwest of Argentina and the Altiplano studying the work of itinerant poets and folk music styles of the indigenous

South American culture. Their cultures and rhythms helped form his original compositions.

Atahualpa wrote his first song, "Caminito del Indio" in 1926. The song introduced his themes of indigenous folk music and protest, along with an intricate fingerpicking style of playing he developed.

The protest and political themes of his songs led him to become active in political circles. He joined the communist party and in 1931 took part in a failed uprising to support the deposed president, Hipólito Yrigoyen. With the defeat of the uprising, Atahualpa fled to Uruguay. He did not return to Argentina until 1934.

Atahualpa first visited Buenos Aires in 1935. His compositions were becoming popular, and they invited him to perform on one of the local radio stations. Soon after this visit, he met the pianist, Antonietta Paula Pepin Fitzpatrick (nicknamed "Nenette").

Nenette became Atahualpa's lifelong musical collaborator, and they married in 1946.

His public attachment to the communist party in the 1940s often put him in disagreement with the Argentine government. They temporarily imprisoned him several times and censored his work.

Disillusioned with Argentina, Atahualpa left for Europe in 1949.

In 1950, Édith Piaf encouraged him to perform in Paris. This was a step toward public recognition, and he often opened for Piaff. During this period, he became friends with many artists, including Picasso, who appreciated his poetry with its themes of poverty and oppression.

Atahualpa signed a contract with the recording company Le Chant du Monde. His first LP (Miner I Am) won the Charles Cros Academy award for best foreign disc. Because of the popularity of the LP, he embarked on an extensive tour of Europe before returning to Buenos Aires.

By 1952, when he returned to Argentina, Atahualpa had broken off affiliations with the Argentinian Communist Party. He now found it easier to get bookings and radio appearances. During this period, Nenette and Atahualpa built their house on Cerro Colorado in Córdoba province. He alternated between houses in Buenos Aires and Cerro Colorado.

His music and popularity grew, and by the 1960s, his compositions were being recorded by Nueva Cancion artists. This led to recognition amongst younger musicians.

Between 1963 and 1964, Atahualpa toured Colombia, Egypt, Morocco, Israel, Italy and Japan.

In 1967, he toured Spain, then settled in Paris. Atahualpa visited Argentina many times over the years. But these visits became less and less when the military dictatorship of Jorge Videla took control of the country in 1976.

The prestigious University of Nanterre contacted Atahualpa in 1989 and asked him to write the lyrics of a cantata to commemorate the bicentennial of the French Revolution, to be released by the French authorities. He entitled the composition "The sacred Word". It is a tribute to the oppressed people that freed themselves during the great struggle.

Atahualpa Yupanqui died in Nimes, France in 1992, aged 84. They dispersed his cremated remains on his beloved Cerro Colorado, on 8 June 1992.

During his career, he recorded over 12,000 songs. We still play many of them every day and I hope my contribution to the ukulele world helps with preserving his legacy.

TECHNIQUES & NOTATION

NAMING CONVENTION FOR HANDS

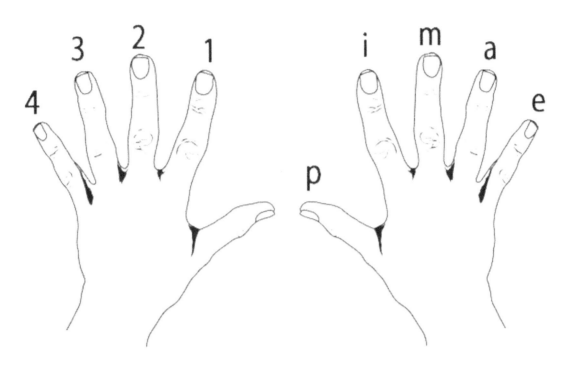

Right Hand

p = pulgar (thumb)
i = indice (index finger/first finger
m = medio (middle finger)
a = ãnular (ring finger/third finger)
e = meñique (little finger/fourth finger)

Guitar music uses p, a, m and i to show right hand fingering but the fourth finger has no standard symbol so I have used 'e' because that was the letter used when I was learning to play Flamenco guitar.

Left Hand

uke.

The image above shows how the left hand numbering is shown in the music. The small numbers in the music show the fingers to use. In the image above, the first finger is on the C string, the second finger is on the E string and the third finger is on the A string.

The fourth finger comes into play to stop the third fret on the A string.

POSITION OF FINGERS

The thumb should be parallel to the strings and strikes the strings with the side of the thumb. In, most instances the thumb plays a rest stroke by pushing downwards until it rests on the next string. When not in use, the thumb rests lightly on the G string or resting on the body of the ukulele and just above the G string.

- ☐ Thumb (p) on the G string (4th string)
- ☐ Index finger on the C String (3rd string)
- ☐ Middle finger on the E string (2nd string)
- ☐ Third finger on the A string (1st string)

The thumb and finger positioning will make the tunes in this book easier to play and it is a good habit to get into no matter what style of ukulele you wish to play.

Get into the habit of positioning your fingers as above, and using those fingers to pluck those strings when two or more strings need to be plucked at the same time.

NOTATION OF FINGER POSITIONS

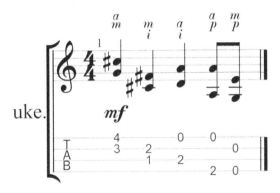

Throughout the book, you will see notation, as shown above in the image.

The small letters above the notes show which fingers to use. If you start with your fingers on (or just above) the strings as shown in the starting position, the fingers will be in the best position to pluck the strings.

Where three fingers are needed to pluck the strings, you have two options, as seen in the next image:

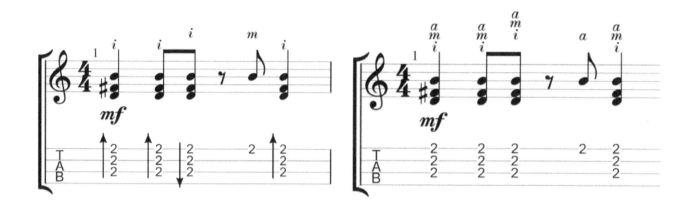

☐ Use the three fingers

☐ Strike the string with your index finger

Using either will give a distinct sound. When I am playing, I will use whichever feels best.

Which finger to use is a preference. But if you get used to having your fingers just above the strings, and use the assigned fingers, as shown in the position of fingers section, your playing will flow. It will sound effortless because you are not thinking about which fingers to use.

ADIOS TUCUMAN

CANCIONES DEL ABEULO NO1

CANCIONES DEL ABEULO NO2

CANCIONES DEL LOS HORNEROS

EL ALAZAN

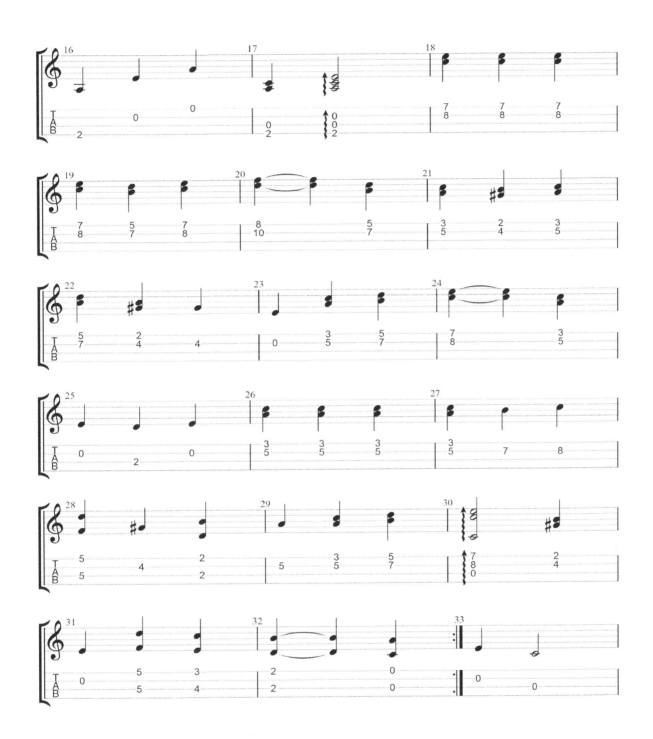

EL AROMO

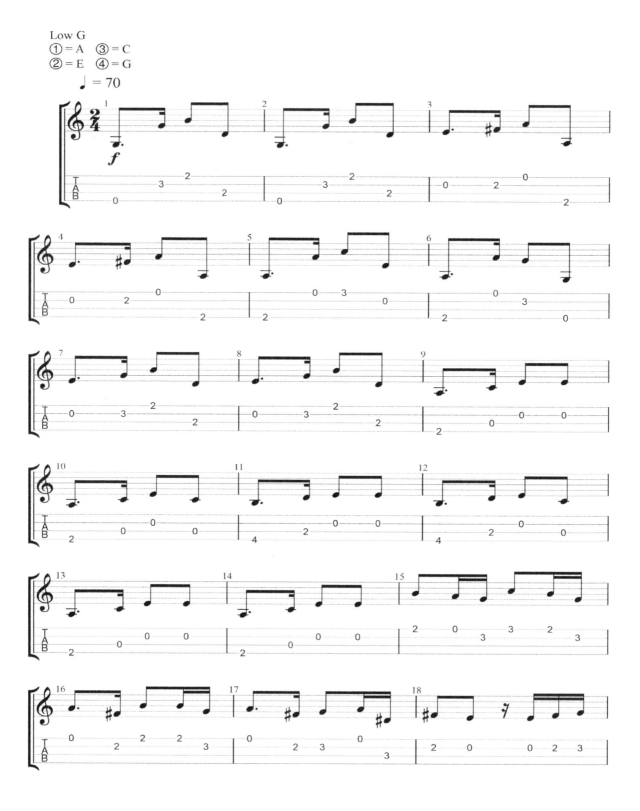

EL ARRIERO

EL INDIO Y LA QUENA

LA DEL CAMPO

LA OLVIDADA

LA POBRECITA

LOS EJES DE MI CARRETA

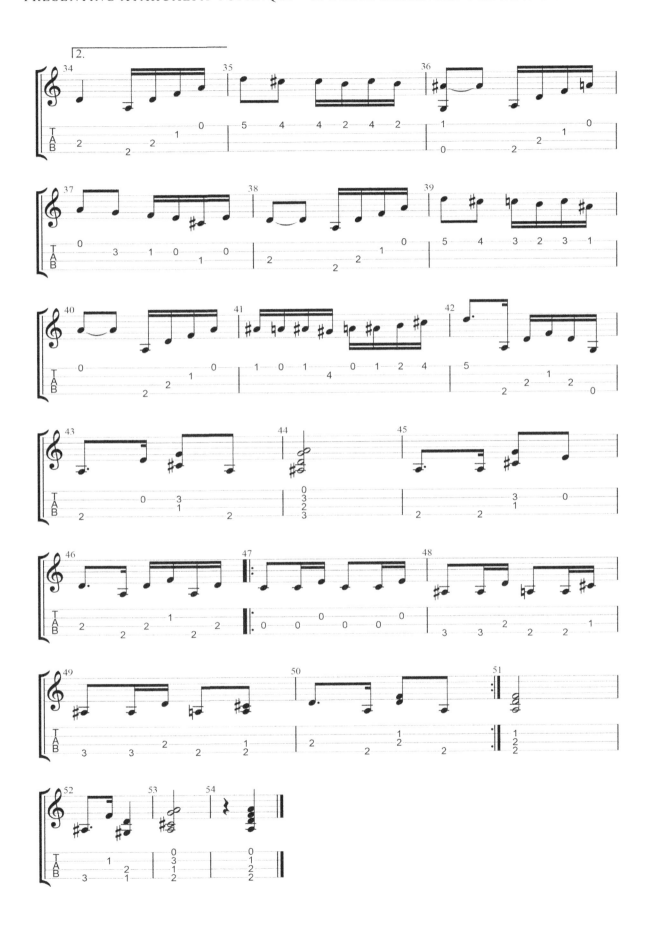

LUNA TUCUMANA

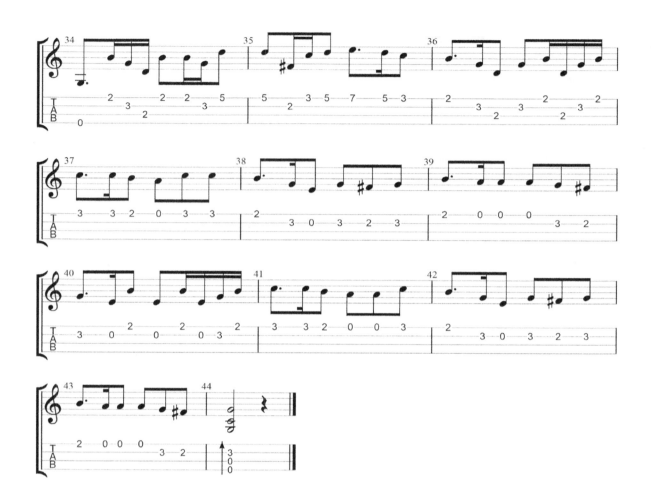

MILONGA DEL SOLITARIO

PIEDRA Y CAMINO

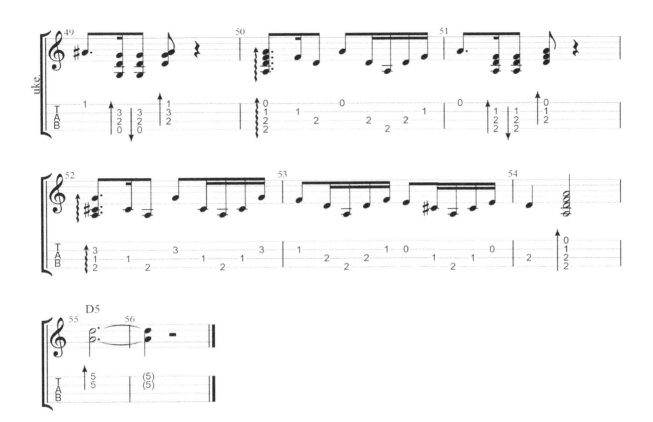

TU QUE PUEDES VUELVETE

ABOUT THE AUTHOR

   I am called Dave Brown and I live in the UK in a picturesque market town in the re-laxed county of Suffolk.

My philosophy has always been to only do things that make me happy, and I have been lucky enough to have achieved this. I traveled the world, following my boyhood dream, with a successful comedy magic act and sleight-of-hand performances until an accident on stage cut short my career.

An unexpected gift of a ukulele from my wife one Christmas awakened a dormant interest in Flamenco. I had played flamenco guitar for several years but it was uncomfortable playing because of my accident and I sidelined the guitar. Because of my newly discovered interest in ukulele, I built a website devoted to Flamenco Ukulele, (www.flamencoukulele.com) so enthusiasts have somewhere to find information.

As a natural offshoot of the website, I wrote and published a series of books, and I continue to bring this finger-picking style to the ukulele playing fraternity.

The music of Atahualpa Yupanqui was an unexpected find. His music captivated me immediately, and I knew I wanted to bring it to the attention of the ukulele playing fraternity.

The resource pack has .pdf documents of the tunes and mp3 files (to help you understand the rhythm of the tune) at a suggested speed. You can download the pack from https://flamencoukulele.com/atahualpa-notes

If you have a moment, please consider leaving your honest feedback as a review. Your feedback helps future customers make an informed decision, and I appreciate any feedback.

FURTHER READING

FLAMENCO UKULELE BOOKS BY THE SAME AUTHOR.

Flamenco Ukulele Solos – book 1

Includes:

- A modern Malagueña by Paco de Lucia
- Traditional Fandangos de Huelva
- Traditional Soleares
- Traditional Verdiales
- Traditional Zapateado

Flamenco Ukulele Solos – book 2

Includes:

- Traditional Alegrias
- Traditional Bulerias
- Traditional Guajiras
- Traditional Panaderos
- Traditional Tanguillos

Flamenco Ukulele Solos – book 3

Includes:

- Traditional Farucca
- Traditional Malagueña
- Traditional Tangos
- Traditional Tientos
- Traditional Zambra

Flamenco Ukulele Solos – The Collection

All of the above Flamenco Solos brought together in one book

Flamenco Ukulele Sevillanas – collection 1

Four traditional Sevillanas

Flamenco Ukulele Sevillanas – collection 2

Four traditional Sevillanas

Flamenco Ukulele Sevillanas – collection 3

Four traditional Sevillanas

Flamenco Ukulele Sevillanas – Ultimate collection

All of the above Sevillanas collections brought together in one book.

Simplified Flamenco Ukulele Rhythms

A short series of books aimed at simplifying the rhythm sections of Flamenco tunes. The rasgueo can be a daunting prospect, using four or five fingers all working in sync can take a long time to achieve. I have developed a method of using just two fingers to achieve a similar sound in a fraction of the time.

Book 1 includes:

- Four Sevillanas
- Tientos
- Verdiales
- Zapateado

Book 2 includes:

- Alegrias
- Fandangos
- Farruca
- Malagueña
- Soleares

Note: Some of the tunes are similar to those in the Flamenco Ukulele Solos series but are shortened versions without the fine detail.

OTHER UKULELE BOOKS BY THE SAME AUTHOR.

Tango

12 Easy to play tango tunes for low G ukulele

Book 1 includes:

- La Cumparsita

- Libertango
- Malena
- Mi Buenos Aires Querido
- Nostalgias
- Por Una Cabeza
- Soledad
- Sus Ojos Se Cerraron
- Tango No. 2
- Tango No. 3
- Tango (Tarrega)
- Valse Venezuelienne

Spanish

15 Spanish tunes for Low G ukulele

Book includes:

- Cajita Da Musica
- Campesina Santandereana
- Cancion O Tocata
- El Cuando
- El Humahuaquerno
- El Jaleo
- Historia De Un Amor
- IV Porro
- Lagrima Negras
- La Media Cana

- Malagueña
- Mi Hamaca
- Molondron
- Scherzino Mexicano
- Una Tarde Fresquita De Mayo

OTHER MUSIC BOOKS BY THE SAME AUTHOR

Tango for Chromatic Harmonica

12 tango tunes arranged for Chromatic harmonica.

Each tune with full music and harmonica tabs. Even if you can't read music, just listen to the tune, follow the numbers and you will play a Tango.

Book 1 includes:

- El Choclo
- Golandrinas
- La Cumparsita
- Malena
- Mi Buenos Aires Querido
- Soledad
- Sus Ojos Se Cerraron
- Tango No. 2
- Tango No. 3
- Tomo y Obligo
- Tango (Tarrega)
- Valse Venezuelienne

Made in the USA
Las Vegas, NV
14 November 2024

GYPSY & FOLK TUNES FROM EASTERN EUROPE

23 tunes arranged for Chromatic harmonica.

Each tune with full music and harmonica tabs. Even if you can't read music, just listen to the tune, follow the numbers and you will play a the tune.

Book 1 includes:

- Bantiki
- Dve Gitary
- Ia Ne Skazhu Tebe
- Khoroshi Vesnoi V Sadu Tsvetochki
- Korobeiniki
- Tsyganochki
- Vizhu Chudnoe Privol'e
- Vsyo Chto Bylo
- Csók Proba
- Hogy Mondjam Meg Néked
- Kalitka
- A Ti Utcátokban Fényesebb A Csillag

- Libamaj Kacsamaj
- Maros Vize Folyik Csendesen
- Sárga Csizmát Visel A Babám
- Szép A Rozsám
- Czech Medley
- Ukrainian Folk Song
- Gypsy 01
- Gypsy 02
- Ne Serdiš'
- Stick Dance
- Vasiločki